Election Results 2024

A Comprehensive Analysis of the Key Outcomes, Voter Shifts, State-by-State Breakdown and how Trump's Won.

Graham Sinclair

Copyright©2024 by [Graham Sinclair]

All rights reserved. No part of this publication may be reproduced, distributed, or transmitted in any form or by any means, including photocopying, recording, or other electronic or mechanical methods, without the prior written permission of the publisher, except in the case of brief quotations embodied in critical reviews and certain other noncommercial uses permitted by copyright law.

TABLE OF CONTENT

Introduction: The 2024 Election in Historical Context............5
   The Stakes of the 2024 Election 5
   The Evolution of Political Strategy and Voter Sentiment 7

Chapter 1: The Road to Election Day 13
   Key Events in the Primary Season..............................13
   Major Campaign Strategies and Themes...........................15

Chapter 2: Key Issues and Voter Concerns 21
   Defining Issues for Voters in 2024 21
   The Impact of Economic and Social Factors 24

Chapter 3: The Trump Strategy 29
   Trump's Messaging and Campaign Themes 29
   Key Voter Outreach Efforts and Ground Strategy 31

Chapter 4: Voter Turnout and Demographic Shifts 37
   Trends in Voter Turnout Across Demographics 37
   Shifts in Support Among Key Voter Groups 40

Chapter 5: Swing States and Decisive Moments......................45
   Analysis of Critical Swing States and Voting Patterns 45
   Pivotal Moments and Campaign Turning Points 47

Chapter 6: State-by-State Analysis................................53
   Notable State Results and Regional Trends......................53
   Key Takeaways from Each State's Voting Outcome 56

Chapter 7: Impact of Voter Sentiment and Media Influence..61
   Role of Traditional and Social Media in Shaping Views 61

Public Sentiment and Key Influencers in the Election 64

Chapter 8: Election Day and the Final Results........................69

    Key Events on Election Day...69

    Breakdown of Final Results and Close Contests...................71

Chapter 9: Reactions from Both Sides...75

    Reactions from Trump Supporters and Opponents 75

    International Responses to the U.S. Election Outcome......78

Chapter 10: What Trump's Win Means for America 83

    Policy Agenda and Expected Legislative Focus....................83

    Anticipated Changes in Domestic and Foreign Policy........86

Chapter 11: Challenges and Opportunities in a New Era 91

    Obstacles Facing the New Administration 91

    Areas for Potential Bipartisan Collaboration 94

Chapter 12: The Future of American Politics Post-2024 99

    Implications for Future Presidential Elections 99

    Shifting Dynamics Within the Major Political Parties.......102

Conclusion: A Defining Election 107

    Long-Term Implications for American Democracy 107

    The Place of the 2024 Election in Political History..............110

Introduction: The 2024 Election in Historical Context

The Stakes of the 2024 Election

The 2024 U.S. Presidential Election was much more than a choice between two candidates; it became a powerful reflection of the country's pressing issues and ideological divides. With Donald Trump making a return to the political scene, running for a second, non-consecutive term, the election was framed as a pivotal point in American history. Trump's re-entry into the political arena stirred the nation, igniting fervent support among his base while prompting opposition among those wary of his governance style. For many Americans, the stakes of this election felt more intense than in previous cycles, as they perceived it as a battle over the soul and future direction of the country.

A backdrop of significant issues added to the gravity of the election. America was grappling with economic uncertainty, societal division, and ongoing global tensions. The lingering effects of the pandemic continued to shape the economy, impacting employment, inflation, and small businesses. Economic stability became a top priority for many voters who felt that rising costs and stagnant wages were making life increasingly difficult. Trump's promise to address these economic concerns through reduced government intervention and tax reforms struck a chord with those feeling left behind by the current system. However, his critics argued that his approach might deepen societal divisions and neglect pressing social issues.

Beyond the economy, other critical issues drove voter sentiment. Climate change was a significant concern, especially among younger and progressive voters. They saw the 2024 election as an opportunity to push for stronger environmental protections, advocating for policies to curb emissions, promote renewable energy, and tackle global warming. On the other side, Trump's supporters tended to prioritise issues like immigration control, national security, and job growth, viewing them as central to maintaining America's strength and sovereignty. This divide in priorities made the stakes feel even higher, as each group feared the consequences of the other's agenda taking precedence.

In addition to these issues, the nature of the candidates themselves amplified the election's importance. Trump's outspoken style and promises of bold change stood in stark contrast to his opponent's message of stability and continuity. For Trump supporters, his return symbolized a leader who was willing to stand up against political correctness and challenge the establishment. His opposition, however, viewed his candidacy as a potential threat to democratic norms, concerned that his approach might undermine institutions and disrupt global alliances. These contrasting views created an election in which voters were not only choosing a president but also endorsing a vision for America's future. The stakes felt personal, and for many, it was an election that would shape the country's identity and trajectory for generations to come.

The Evolution of Political Strategy and Voter Sentiment

Over the past decade, political strategy in the United States has evolved rapidly, driven by advances in technology, changing media landscapes, and shifting voter expectations. By 2024, campaigns were more data-driven and targeted than ever before, allowing candidates to reach specific demographics with tailored messages that resonated with their concerns. This evolution in strategy reflected a growing understanding of the nuanced needs of the electorate, allowing campaigns to focus on the issues that mattered most to key voting blocs. In the 2024 election, both Trump and his opponent leveraged these modern tactics to influence and mobilise their supporters.

Trump's campaign, in particular, demonstrated a deep understanding of his base, using direct and often provocative messaging to tap into feelings of frustration and disillusionment among working-class and rural voters. His strategy was built on the notion that many Americans felt alienated by political elites and were looking for a leader who would champion their interests without concern for traditional norms. By crafting messages that resonated with their sense of identity and pride, Trump's campaign fostered a connection that went beyond policy, creating a movement centered around his persona. This approach was amplified through targeted social media campaigns, which allowed his team to reach millions with specific messages that reinforced loyalty and energised supporters.

In contrast, his opponent's campaign aimed to appeal to a broader coalition, focusing on inclusivity, environmental action, and stability. Their strategy relied heavily on grassroots support and outreach to younger voters, minority communities, and urban populations who were motivated by social justice and climate issues. They used sophisticated data analysis to understand what issues drove their supporters, using this information to craft messages that aligned with progressive values. Social media also played a vital role here, as the campaign used platforms to mobilise these groups, leveraging influencers and digital ads to reach young voters who may not have engaged with traditional political content.

Voter sentiment, shaped by both economic concerns and cultural divides, also evolved in recent years, leading to an electorate that was more vocal and polarised. Issues like economic inequality, healthcare access, and climate action had taken centre stage, largely driven by younger generations who expected leaders to address these concerns with urgency. This generational shift was apparent in the 2024 election, as younger voters pushed for progressive policies, environmental protections, and equality. Many of these voters were highly engaged and willing to use their voices to demand change, challenging the traditional norms of political engagement.

Meanwhile, other demographics, especially those in rural and industrial areas, felt that these progressive issues did not address their everyday struggles. For them, job security, national pride, and border control were at the forefront. This divide created a unique electoral landscape, where campaigns needed to address highly specific concerns within diverse voter blocs. Trump's emphasis on "America First" resonated strongly with those who felt that globalization and progressive policies had left them behind. This divide was not just ideological but emotional, as each group saw their vision of America at odds with the other's.

The role of media and information dissemination also evolved in this context. Traditional media had been gradually overshadowed by social media and independent news platforms, which allowed individuals to curate their information sources according to their beliefs. As a result, echo chambers became more prominent, with people receiving news that reinforced their views while limiting exposure to opposing perspectives. This development influenced voter sentiment by intensifying polarization and shaping perceptions of each candidate based on curated narratives. In 2024, this trend was evident as social media algorithms delivered content that aligned with users' political leanings, creating divided realities where each side felt validated in their beliefs.

This evolution of political strategy and voter sentiment ultimately made the 2024 election a defining moment in American democracy. Campaigns had moved beyond broad, generic messages and focused on micro-targeting, influencing specific groups with precisely crafted narratives. This approach demonstrated the power of modern political strategy, where understanding voter sentiment and addressing their unique concerns had become the cornerstone of electoral success. The heightened stakes of the election were a direct result of these shifts, as each side believed that their chosen candidate was the only viable option for the future of the nation.

As the election unfolded, it became clear that these strategic shifts and the evolution of voter sentiment were reshaping the fabric of American politics. The ability of campaigns to directly engage voters through data-driven messages and social media platforms highlighted both the possibilities and the challenges of modern democracy. On one hand, these methods allowed for more personalized engagement, potentially empowering voters by addressing their specific concerns. On the other hand, it intensified divisions by creating insular spaces where opposing viewpoints were often dismissed or ignored.

In the historical context of the 2024 election, the stakes were intensified by this transformation of political engagement. Voters were not only more aware of the power of their vote but also more deeply entrenched in their beliefs, viewing the election as a choice between two radically different futures for America. This atmosphere of urgency and division will likely be remembered as a key characteristic of the 2024 election, marking it as one of the most consequential elections in recent history.

Chapter 1: The Road to Election Day

Key Events in the Primary Season

The primary season for the 2024 U.S. Presidential Election set the stage for a contentious and highly anticipated race, one that brought familiar faces and emerging voices to the forefront of American politics. As the primaries unfolded, each candidate worked to secure their place on the ballot by winning over both core supporters and undecided voters. For Donald Trump, the path to the Republican nomination was marked by both resilience and controversy. His re-entry into the political arena, aiming for a second non-consecutive term, immediately reshaped the Republican primary landscape. While other contenders, including prominent figures within the party, attempted to challenge his influence, Trump's established base and magnetic appeal among voters positioned him as a frontrunner from the outset.

The Republican primaries became a defining moment, as Trump navigated debates and campaign stops with a strategy honed from his previous political experience. Early in the season, he faced challenges from within his own party, particularly from those who had become critical of his policies or leadership style since his first term. However, Trump's ability to tap into the sentiments of his supporters—emphasizing an America-first agenda and a return to conservative values—helped him solidify his standing, even as critics questioned his suitability for a second term. This period also saw significant media attention, as Trump's every move was scrutinised, with analysts debating whether he could recapture the momentum that brought him to victory in 2016.

The Democratic primaries, meanwhile, saw their own share of challenges and developments. With the incumbent administration aiming to secure a continued hold on the presidency, the Democratic field was focused on promoting stability, continuity, and policy reforms that appealed to their base. However, internal debates and ideological differences within the party highlighted a growing divide between moderate and progressive factions. Each candidate worked to appeal to the concerns of various demographic groups, addressing issues ranging from economic reform and healthcare to climate change and social justice. The Democratic primary season was marked by spirited debates and the effort to unify the party around a message that could counter Trump's assertive return.

The primary season culminated in a set of defining events, from televised debates that showcased the policies and personalities of each candidate to the endorsements that followed. Trump's dominance in the Republican primaries confirmed his command over his base, while the Democratic field worked to establish a vision of stability and progressive reform. These months of campaigning, strategizing, and debating were crucial in shaping the narratives that would follow both candidates into the general election, as each prepared to capture the attention of the wider electorate in the months leading up to November.

Major Campaign Strategies and Themes

As the general election season unfolded, the campaign strategies employed by each candidate highlighted the sharp contrast between Trump's bold approach and his opponent's focus on continuity and progressive reform. Trump's campaign strategy was both familiar and refined, building on the themes he had championed in his previous term but with a renewed emphasis on what he framed as unfinished business. His central message was a call to "Make America Great Again, Again," signalling a return to the policies and priorities he had advocated during his first term. Trump focused on rallying his core supporters, using his characteristic directness and assertiveness to appeal to those who felt disillusioned by recent political trends.

One of Trump's primary strategies was to position himself as the candidate who would challenge the status quo, taking a strong stand on issues such as immigration, national security, and economic independence. His messaging was crafted to resonate with voters who were frustrated with what they perceived as overreach from the federal government and sought a leader who would prioritise American interests above all. Trump's campaign rallies, often marked by large crowds and intense energy, served as focal points where he could connect with his supporters directly, delivering messages that reinforced his commitment to them. His team also harnessed social media effectively, using targeted ads and posts to mobilise his base and counter criticisms from opponents.

His opponent's campaign leaned into themes of stability, unity, and progressive reform, aimed at appealing to a diverse coalition of voters across demographic lines. The opposing campaign sought to project an image of steady leadership, with an emphasis on continuity and the belief that incremental progress was the path forward for the nation. Recognising the concerns of younger voters and progressive groups, the campaign promoted policies on climate action, healthcare reform, and social equity. These messages were carefully tailored to attract a broad coalition, from young urban voters to suburban families concerned about healthcare and the environment.

The thematic contrasts between the campaigns were evident in both their messaging and outreach. Trump's strategy capitalized on populist themes, positioning himself as a candidate who would defend American values against both foreign and domestic threats. His opponent, by contrast, presented a vision of a country moving forward collectively, with a focus on addressing societal inequalities and adapting to modern challenges. This divergence in themes was not only a reflection of their differing visions for the country but also an indication of the ideological divides that had become increasingly pronounced in American politics.

Both campaigns invested heavily in digital advertising, recognising the power of targeted messages to reach specific voter groups. Trump's team targeted rural and working-class areas with messages focused on job creation, national pride, and border security, while the opposition campaign targeted urban and suburban areas with messages on healthcare, education, and social justice. The use of data analytics allowed each campaign to refine their messages and reach undecided voters with appeals tailored to their concerns. This approach underscored the evolution of campaign strategy, with data-driven decisions becoming central to modern political tactics.

As the election drew closer, these strategies intensified, with each candidate doubling down on their core themes. Trump's campaign focused on energizing his base, using language and messaging that emphasised strength, resilience, and a commitment to restoring what he saw as the values that had made America great. His opponent's campaign, meanwhile, focused on unity and inclusivity, appealing to voters' hopes for a stable and progressive future. This contrast was highlighted in debates, public appearances, and advertisements, creating a clear choice for voters between two distinct visions for the country.

The road to Election Day was marked by these contrasting strategies, as each campaign sought to capture the support of an electorate increasingly divided along ideological lines. Trump's base, drawn to his assertive style and commitment to conservative values, contrasted sharply with those who supported a vision of progressivism and unity.

The 2024 election became not only a contest of personalities but a competition between two deeply rooted visions for America's future. As the candidates made their final appeals to voters, the campaign strategies and themes they had cultivated throughout the season would prove decisive in shaping the outcome of one of the most critical elections in American history.

Chapter 2: Key Issues and Voter Concerns

Defining Issues for Voters in 2024

The 2024 election was driven by a set of key issues that profoundly resonated with the electorate, shaping their choices and intensifying the political landscape. At the forefront were concerns about economic stability, healthcare, and the role of government, with each issue impacting voters across a wide range of demographics. Economic concerns were especially significant as Americans grappled with the long-term impacts of inflation, rising costs of living, and employment uncertainty. For many, the economy was not an abstract concern but a daily reality, influencing everything from household budgets to career opportunities and financial security. The candidates each offered starkly different approaches to addressing these challenges, giving voters clear, if polarising, options.

Healthcare remained a defining issue, as voters voiced concerns about access, affordability, and the quality of services. The legacy of pandemic-related disruptions to the healthcare system left many Americans feeling vulnerable, with gaps in care and long wait times becoming increasingly common.

Rising healthcare costs further complicated this landscape, particularly for working families and seniors who struggled to keep up with medical expenses. Trump's approach to healthcare, which promised reforms to reduce bureaucracy and lower costs, appealed to those who felt underserved by the current system. In contrast, his opponent emphasised expanding access and providing government-backed solutions, catering to voters who believed in the importance of a comprehensive safety net. This contrast underscored a broader ideological divide over the role of government in ensuring access to essential services.

Climate change emerged as a crucial issue, particularly among younger voters and progressives. For many, the urgency of environmental issues had reached a peak, with climate-related events such as wildfires, floods, and extreme weather bringing the reality of global warming closer to home. Young voters, in particular, pushed for immediate action, demanding policies to curb carbon emissions, invest in renewable energy, and hold corporations accountable for their environmental impact. Trump's stance on climate policy, which favored energy independence and deregulation, appealed to voters concerned about energy costs and job creation, especially in energy-producing regions. His opponent's platform, which focused on renewable energy investments and stricter environmental regulations, resonated with voters committed to environmental protection and long-term sustainability.

Social justice and equity also remained pivotal issues in 2024, reflecting the shifting dynamics of a diverse and increasingly vocal society. Issues such as racial equality, LGBTQ+ rights, and gender equality became focal points, with activists and advocacy groups urging candidates to address systemic inequities. Trump's campaign strategy leaned towards a focus on law and order, resonating with voters who felt that social stability was at risk. His opponent's platform, which highlighted reforms aimed at addressing discrimination and inequality, resonated with communities and allies seeking substantial social change. These issues, deeply rooted in personal identity and experience, played a significant role in shaping voter sentiment and drove engagement among groups who felt that their voices had been marginalised in previous election cycles.

The Impact of Economic and Social Factors

The economic and social landscape of 2024 played a critical role in determining voter priorities and guiding the narrative of the election. Economic uncertainty was one of the most pressing issues for Americans, many of whom had experienced stagnant wages, inflation, and a housing market that seemed increasingly out of reach. For working-class and middle-class families, the challenge of meeting basic needs had become a central concern, and the rising costs of essential items such as food, fuel, and housing compounded the feeling of financial instability. Trump's campaign addressed these concerns by promising to reduce government interference, cut taxes, and boost American manufacturing, framing his platform as a pathway to economic revitalisation. This message resonated particularly well with voters in industrial areas and rural communities, who believed that government policies had disadvantaged them in favour of urban and coastal elites.

Social factors also played a crucial role in shaping the priorities of the electorate. The pandemic had highlighted inequalities in access to resources and services, making social equity a prominent issue for many voters. Communities that had been disproportionately affected by the pandemic—whether through job losses, health disparities, or limited access to digital resources—sought policies that would address these systemic inequities. Trump's focus on individual freedom and his approach to reducing what he termed as "government overreach" appealed to voters who prioritised personal choice over institutional intervention. His opponent's focus on social safety nets and community support, however, attracted those who believed that government had a responsibility to level the playing field, ensuring that all citizens had access to the resources they needed to thrive.

Housing affordability became another defining factor in 2024, with homeownership increasingly out of reach for younger generations and urban renters facing skyrocketing costs. The impact of housing issues was particularly pronounced in cities where demand continued to outpace supply, driving up prices and creating a sense of instability for many. Trump's promise to deregulate and stimulate job growth appealed to voters who felt that economic stimulation would provide pathways to homeownership and financial stability. His opponent's proposals to expand affordable housing and provide assistance for renters resonated with younger voters and urban residents who felt that the housing market was unfairly structured in favour of established homeowners and corporations.

One of the subtler but equally influential social factors was the shift in generational priorities and values. Younger voters, who had grown up in an era of rapid technological advancement, environmental awareness, and social movements, brought new perspectives to the electoral landscape. For many of these voters, traditional concerns about job security and national security were accompanied by a deep commitment to addressing climate change, promoting social justice, and fostering an inclusive society. Trump's campaign, which focused on traditional economic and security issues, appealed more strongly to older generations and working-class communities. His opponent's platform, by contrast, sought to engage these younger voters with promises of climate action, education reform, and expanded healthcare.

The role of information access also emerged as a defining factor in 2024, with social media and digital platforms continuing to influence how people received news and understood issues. As in previous elections, social media played a dual role: it mobilized young voters, connecting them with advocacy movements and empowering them to push for change, but it also created echo chambers where misinformation could spread rapidly. Economic and social concerns were often amplified by these platforms, where specific issues could gain traction and shape public perception in powerful ways. For instance, concerns over healthcare and inflation circulated widely, influencing voters' views and sometimes polarising debates further. Social media allowed voters to engage with issues directly, yet also exposed them to partisan narratives that reinforced existing biases.

The intersection of economic and social issues in 2024 created a complex voting landscape, where individuals weighed their personal experiences against the broader vision presented by each candidate. Economic instability had a direct impact on social cohesion, with many Americans feeling that their ability to participate in society was increasingly constrained by financial pressures. This feeling was especially pronounced among working families and small business owners, who often felt disconnected from the broader economic growth touted by politicians. Trump's economic promises appealed to these voters by emphasizing self-reliance and the potential for individual success, while his opponent's platform aimed to create structural supports that would address these systemic barriers.

The 2024 election was defined by a confluence of economic and social factors that collectively shaped voter concerns. The defining issues—healthcare, the economy, climate, and social justice—reflected a divided society grappling with questions of identity, security, and fairness. Voters approached these issues not just as abstract policies, but as real, tangible concerns that impacted their daily lives and futures. The outcome of the election, therefore, became more than a question of leadership; it was a reflection of the country's values and priorities, embodying the complex and evolving nature of the American political landscape. Each side saw their candidate not only as a leader but as a champion for the issues that mattered most to them, making the stakes higher and the divisions deeper than ever before.

Chapter 3: The Trump Strategy

Trump's Messaging and Campaign Themes

In the 2024 election, Donald Trump's campaign centred around a distinctive and sharply focused messaging strategy. Known for his direct, sometimes controversial style, Trump refined his approach to resonate with his core base while also appealing to undecided voters who were concerned about the state of the economy, national security, and American sovereignty. Trump's messaging was grounded in familiar themes, emphasizing his "America First" policy, which prioritised American interests over global partnerships. This approach struck a chord with voters who felt disillusioned by what they saw as decades of foreign entanglements and trade deals that, in their view, left American workers and businesses at a disadvantage.

Economic resilience and job growth were central to Trump's campaign themes. As inflation and the cost of living rose in recent years, Trump focused heavily on the promise of an economically prosperous America, aiming to restore confidence in the country's financial future. He promised policies that would reduce regulation, cut taxes for middle- and working-class Americans, and bring back manufacturing jobs that many believed had been outsourced. For Trump, these economic promises were not just policies but symbols of his commitment to the average American worker. His speeches often targeted blue-collar workers, emphasizing that he understood their struggles and would work to restore their prosperity.

Another core theme in Trump's campaign was border security. He reinforced his stance on immigration, advocating for strict border policies and an increased focus on national security. He argued that without controlled borders, American resources and jobs were at risk, and he made clear promises to curb illegal immigration, expand the border wall, and enforce immigration laws more rigorously. This theme resonated with voters who were concerned about immigration's impact on their communities, job security, and social services. Trump's commitment to "build the wall" became a rallying cry that symbolized his promise to protect American interests and maintain sovereignty.

National pride and the defence of American values were equally pivotal in Trump's messaging. He often spoke about restoring traditional values, portraying his administration as a defender of American heritage and cultural norms. This theme appealed particularly to voters who felt alienated by progressive social changes and who feared that the American identity they cherished was being diluted. Trump emphasised that his leadership was a stand against what he described as "woke" culture and policies that, in his view, divided Americans rather than uniting them. By framing himself as a protector of American values, Trump reinforced his image as a champion of the people, creating a strong bond with voters who felt that their voices and concerns were ignored by political elites.

Key Voter Outreach Efforts and Ground Strategy

Trump's ground strategy in 2024 was more targeted and sophisticated than ever, employing a well-coordinated outreach effort that focused on maximizing voter engagement, particularly in battleground states. Unlike previous campaigns that relied heavily on large rallies and broad media appeals, Trump's 2024 team implemented a data-driven approach that allowed them to identify and reach specific voter segments with tailored messaging. Leveraging technology, the campaign used analytics to pinpoint areas with potential swing voters, enabling them to deploy resources strategically and increase support in critical regions.

One of the campaign's main outreach strategies was door-to-door canvassing and localized events in small communities, where Trump's supporters felt seen and heard. This approach was effective in rural and suburban areas, where personal interactions often have a stronger impact than social media ads or television spots. Trump's team worked to connect with local leaders, community organisations, and grassroots supporters, encouraging them to participate in the campaign's outreach efforts. By mobilizing people from within the community to advocate on his behalf, Trump's campaign fostered a sense of ownership and personal investment among his supporters, making his platform feel more like a shared mission than a top-down political message.

Social media continued to be an essential tool for Trump's outreach, though his team adapted to the shifting landscape of digital platforms and changing algorithms. His campaign made strategic use of newer platforms to reach younger and more tech-savvy voters who might not be as engaged with traditional news outlets. At the same time, they tailored their messages to fit the distinct culture of each platform, ensuring that content was engaging, relatable, and capable of spreading virally. Trump's presence on social media allowed him to communicate directly with his followers, bypassing traditional media filters and giving him control over his narrative. This direct line to supporters also helped him energies his base, as his posts and videos often went viral, reinforcing loyalty and driving engagement across platforms.

In addition to social media, Trump's team also utilized targeted digital advertising, using voter data to tailor ads that addressed specific concerns within different demographics. For example, ads targeting blue-collar workers might focus on job growth and trade policies, while ads directed at younger voters emphasised economic opportunity and national pride. By personalizing these messages, the campaign managed to make a more profound impact, as voters felt that Trump's platform aligned with their specific needs and aspirations. These digital ads allowed the campaign to reach a vast audience quickly and cost-effectively, solidifying support in areas where Trump's presence on the ground was less practical.

Traditional media was also a component of Trump's outreach, though it was handled differently from previous campaigns. Rather than relying on broad national broadcasts, Trump's campaign worked with local news stations to ensure coverage of his rallies and events in key regions. By focusing on local media, Trump's team reached audiences that national networks might overlook, reinforcing his connection to local issues and the specific concerns of regional communities. This approach helped balance his broader messaging, showing voters that he was committed to addressing issues that affected them directly, not just on a national scale.

Trump's outreach efforts were underpinned by a strong volunteer base that his campaign cultivated with precision. Volunteers were not only tasked with canvassing and distributing materials but were also encouraged to build a sense of community among supporters. The campaign organised events for volunteers that fostered camaraderie, making them feel part of something larger. These volunteers, motivated by a shared commitment to Trump's vision, worked tirelessly to spread his message, often going above and beyond to ensure maximum voter engagement. Trump's ability to inspire such dedication among his base became a significant asset in the 2024 election, as volunteers became both messengers and mobilisers, spreading enthusiasm and turning out voters.

The 2024 campaign also prioritised outreach to minority communities, addressing the perception that Trump's base was predominantly white and rural. His team made concerted efforts to engage with Hispanic and African American voters, especially in swing states where these groups held significant influence. Through targeted ads, events, and partnerships with local community leaders, Trump's campaign sought to present his platform as beneficial to a diverse electorate. While his approach to minority outreach was sometimes viewed as unconventional, the campaign worked to communicate that economic opportunity, national security, and American pride were universal values that transcended racial and ethnic lines.

In the final stretch of the campaign, Trump's team intensified their efforts with a "Get Out the Vote" initiative that involved phone banks, text message reminders, and ride-to-the-polls services. This ground-level operation proved essential in battleground states, where even a slight increase in turnout could influence the outcome. By focusing on logistical support, Trump's campaign aimed to remove any obstacles that might prevent his supporters from voting. The "Get Out the Vote" effort underscored the campaign's commitment to leaving no stone unturned, ensuring that every possible vote was counted.

Through these voter outreach efforts and strategic ground operations, Trump's 2024 campaign demonstrated an evolved approach, blending traditional methods with data-driven innovation. His messaging and ground strategy reflected a deep understanding of his supporters and their concerns, making his campaign not only a bid for the presidency but a movement that resonated with millions of Americans.

Chapter 4: Voter Turnout and Demographic Shifts

Trends in Voter Turnout Across Demographics

The 2024 election saw voter turnout levels that reflected the intense interest and deep-seated convictions among the American electorate. With significant issues at stake, including the economy, social justice, climate action, and national security, voters across demographics were mobilized to make their voices heard. The high turnout was not uniform across all groups, however, and examining these trends provides critical insights into the shifting political landscape.

Older voters, particularly those aged 50 and above, demonstrated a strong turnout rate, motivated largely by concerns over economic stability, healthcare access, and national security. These issues were of heightened importance to them as they face retirement and healthcare needs and are generally more vulnerable to the impacts of economic downturns. Older Americans turned out at consistently high rates, aligning in many cases with conservative policies that prioritised economic independence and limited government intervention.

This group's stability in turnout remains one of the more predictable elements of American voting patterns, with their preferences often reflecting traditional values and a focus on financial security.

On the other hand, younger voters, particularly those under the age of 30, marked a significant demographic shift in the 2024 election. They turned out in substantial numbers, surpassing turnout rates from previous election cycles. The issues driving younger voters included climate change, social justice, and educational reforms. This group is more likely to embrace progressive ideals, viewing government as a force for social change and equity. Their enthusiasm was particularly evident in urban centres and college towns, where organisations and grassroots campaigns targeted youth engagement, registering new voters and encouraging political activism. These voters have been labelled as agents of change, with a passionate belief in addressing systemic issues and advancing progressive policies. Their growing turnout represents a notable demographic shift, underscoring their increasing influence on the political stage.

Minority groups, including Black, Hispanic, and Asian-American communities, also played a vital role in the 2024 election, showing strong levels of participation in areas where voter outreach initiatives were well-coordinated. Black voters, in particular, demonstrated high turnout in urban centres, where the issues of racial equity, police reform, and economic opportunity were at the forefront of political dialogue. Hispanic voters, while diverse in political views, showed considerable engagement, especially in states like Texas, Arizona, and Florida, where immigration policy and economic opportunity were highly relevant. Asian-American voters, a steadily growing segment, also turned out in higher numbers, driven by issues related to education, healthcare, and social justice.

The trends in turnout across these demographics reveal a growing engagement among groups that have historically been underrepresented. While older, white, rural voters maintained strong turnout rates, younger and minority voters increasingly contributed to the electoral outcome. This dynamic reflects the evolving nature of American society, where diverse voices are emerging as influential forces. Campaigns that effectively reached these groups through targeted messaging and community engagement saw tangible results, underscoring the importance of understanding demographic nuances within the electorate. As these trends continue, they are likely to reshape the way future campaigns are strategized, recognising the power of a diverse and engaged voter base.

Shifts in Support Among Key Voter Groups

The 2024 election was not only characterised by high turnout but also by notable shifts in support across key voter groups. These shifts reveal the evolving allegiances and changing priorities within the American electorate. Many groups that had traditionally aligned with one political party began to show new tendencies, reflecting the impact of both the candidates' policies and the issues that dominated the election cycle. These shifts provide a window into the changing preferences and values that are reshaping American politics.

One of the most significant shifts occurred among suburban voters, a group that has historically been a battleground for both major parties. Suburban areas, which are home to a mix of moderate, conservative, and progressive voters, showed a noticeable trend toward the Republican candidate in 2024. Concerns over crime, economic uncertainty, and educational policies played a substantial role in this shift. Many suburban voters, particularly those with families, felt that conservative policies offered a more secure and stable environment for their communities. This trend marked a departure from previous cycles, where suburban areas had learned more Democratic, signalling a re-evaluation of priorities in these increasingly influential regions.

Working-class voters, especially those in industrial and rural areas, also reinforced their support for Trump in the 2024 election. Many in this demographic felt that Trump's policies aligned more closely with their economic needs, focusing on job creation, manufacturing, and reducing international trade agreements that they perceived as harmful to American workers. Trump's promises to revitalize American industry and bring jobs back to U.S. soil resonated deeply with these voters, who saw his approach as a direct response to their economic struggles. This shift solidified Trump's connection with blue-collar workers, creating a loyal base that values his emphasis on "America First" economic policies.

However, shifts among younger, college-educated voters leaned more heavily toward progressive ideals. This group showed increased support for candidates promoting climate action, social equality, and healthcare reform. Many of these voters felt that progressive policies better addressed their concerns about the future, including environmental sustainability, student debt, and social justice. This demographic, often concentrated in urban and metropolitan areas, represented a powerful force advocating for systemic change. Their growing preference for progressive candidates highlights a shift in values among younger voters, who view issues like climate change and economic inequality as critical to their long-term well-being.

There was also a notable shift among Hispanic voters, a diverse group with a range of political views. In 2024, Hispanic support split more evenly than in previous cycles, with a significant portion supporting Trump, particularly in states like Florida and Texas. For many, economic policies and immigration reform were central issues, and Trump's stance on job growth and border security resonated with a segment of Hispanic voters who valued economic stability and conservative social policies.

This shift indicates that Hispanic voters cannot be categorized by a single political ideology and that their support can vary widely depending on regional and cultural factors.

Black voters, a group that has traditionally leaned Democratic, showed increased political engagement, though with some indications of varied support. While many Black voters continued to support progressive candidates, motivated by issues such as police reform and racial justice, a segment showed interest in conservative policies related to economic opportunity and educational reform. This nuanced shift suggests that Black voters are not a monolithic group and that their support may fluctuate based on specific issues and candidate platforms.

The shifts in support among these key voter groups reflect a complex and evolving political landscape. The 2024 election underscored the importance of addressing the unique needs and priorities of each demographic, as voters are increasingly drawn to candidates who resonate with their personal and community values. These shifts highlight the fluidity of American politics, where allegiance to a single party is no longer guaranteed. Instead, voters are more likely to make decisions based on policies that align with their immediate concerns and long-term aspirations.

As these demographic shifts continue to unfold, they will likely have lasting implications for future elections. Political parties may find themselves adjusting their platforms and messaging to accommodate the evolving preferences of these groups, recognising that traditional assumptions about voter loyalty are becoming less reliable. The 2024 election thus serves as a reminder of the diverse and dynamic nature of the American electorate, where shifts in support can redefine the political landscape and shape the direction of the nation's future.

Chapter 5: Swing States and Decisive Moments

Analysis of Critical Swing States and Voting Patterns

The role of swing states in American presidential elections has been pivotal for decades, and the 2024 election was no exception. These states, often balancing between Democratic and Republican support, hold the potential to determine the election's outcome. In 2024, they once again played a crucial role, with candidates pouring resources, time, and targeted messaging into these battlegrounds. The political landscape in states like Pennsylvania, Michigan, Wisconsin, Arizona, and Georgia became focal points for both campaigns, with each candidate understanding that victories in these key areas would be instrumental to securing the presidency.

An analysis of voting patterns across these swing states revealed unique dynamics and shifting demographics that influenced the results. In states such as Pennsylvania and Michigan, there was a noticeable split between urban and rural voters, a pattern consistent with previous elections. Urban areas with diverse populations tended to support progressive policies and Democratic candidates, focusing on issues like climate change, healthcare, and social justice. Meanwhile, rural regions, which have historically leaned conservative, prioritised economic concerns, job security, and issues related to immigration and national security. Trump's strategy capitalized on these rural concerns, tailoring his message to resonate with voters who felt marginalised by more liberal policies.

In the Midwest, Michigan and Wisconsin presented interesting shifts in voter sentiment. These states, which were narrowly won by Trump in 2016 but swung back to the Democrats in 2020, became critical tests of loyalty in 2024. Trump's campaign focused on economic policies aimed at revitalising manufacturing and supporting the working class, tapping into the nostalgia of an industrial past. His message resonated with voters in these areas, where economic anxieties about globalization and automation have left many feeling uncertain about their future. Additionally, Trump's stance on trade and his promise to prioritise American industries struck a chord, swaying key voting blocs within these states and allowing him to make gains that proved instrumental to his success.

On the other hand, states like Arizona and Georgia, once solidly conservative, have shown gradual shifts in their voting demographics. Urban centres in Arizona, especially around Phoenix, and in Georgia, particularly in Atlanta, have seen growing populations of younger, more diverse voters who are increasingly leaning Democratic. This shift posed a challenge for Trump's campaign, which needed to bridge the gap between its traditional base and the more moderate suburban voters. While Trump managed to hold a significant portion of his rural base in these states, the outcome in these areas demonstrated the changing demographics that could impact future elections. The balancing act in Arizona and Georgia highlighted the ongoing transformation of the American political landscape, with suburban and urban voters becoming more influential in historically conservative regions.

Pivotal Moments and Campaign Turning Points

Beyond voting patterns, pivotal moments throughout the campaign defined the direction of the 2024 election, shaping public opinion and impacting the momentum of each candidate. One of the earliest turning points came during the primary season, where intense debates over economic policy, healthcare, and foreign relations revealed the ideological divides within each party. For Trump, the path to nomination involved securing his base while appealing to undecided voters who had not fully embraced his previous administration. His primary campaign, marked by assertive rhetoric and a strong stance on reducing government intervention, set the tone for his general election strategy. This early phase demonstrated his commitment to returning to his original message of economic growth and national pride, consolidating his base and reassuring those who had previously supported him.

As the general election progressed, key moments in debates and campaign rallies also influenced voter sentiment. One significant moment occurred during a debate where Trump highlighted his plans to overhaul government bureaucracy, citing the need to streamline operations and reduce spending. This message resonated with voters who were concerned about government inefficiency and spending, framing him as a candidate committed to fiscal responsibility. On the other hand, his opponent emphasised the importance of social programs and climate initiatives, appealing to voters who prioritised progressive change. These contrasting views on governance gave voters a clear choice, each candidate presenting a distinct vision for the future of the nation.

Another decisive moment came with Trump's outreach to younger voters and independents, where he addressed topics such as freedom of expression, government regulation, and economic opportunity. His emphasis on job creation and reducing government overreach appealed to those concerned about the cost of living and employment opportunities. However, his handling of social issues created a divide, as some voters felt that his focus on economic conservatism lacked the inclusivity they sought. These moments in the campaign highlighted the challenges each candidate faced in appealing to a diverse electorate, with Trump aiming to secure his core base while attracting undecided voters through economic promises.

Social media also played a significant role in shaping the campaign, as key moments were amplified through viral clips and posts that reached millions. Trump's team used platforms like Twitter and Facebook to engage with voters directly, bypassing traditional media filters and connecting with his supporters on a personal level. This strategy allowed his campaign to respond quickly to news developments, counteract criticism, and reinforce his key messages. His digital presence served as a rallying point for supporters, creating a sense of community and momentum that carried through to Election Day. This level of direct engagement proved invaluable in swing states, where voters often felt disconnected from the broader political narrative. By making his messages accessible and relatable, Trump effectively reinforced his appeal to those who felt their voices were overlooked.

Moreover, local issues within swing states became focal points that influenced the outcome of the election. In Pennsylvania, for example, debates around energy policy and job creation became central to the narrative, as the state's economy is heavily reliant on industries like coal and natural gas. Trump's pro-energy stance resonated with voters who feared job losses and economic downturns from stringent environmental policies. Similarly, in Michigan and Wisconsin, his promises to support American manufacturing and reduce reliance on foreign imports struck a chord with working-class voters who felt left behind by globalization. These localized issues, tailored to the needs and concerns of each swing state, created moments that resonated deeply with specific demographics, giving Trump the edge needed to secure victories in key areas.

Finally, Election Day itself was marked by decisive moments as voters turned out in large numbers, driven by the high stakes and polarising nature of the election. Reports of high voter turnout in suburban and rural areas underscored the intensity of the campaign's reach. In states like Georgia and Arizona, the outcome was closely watched, as shifts in suburban voter preferences hinted at changing allegiances. Meanwhile, the results in the Rust Belt states reaffirmed Trump's stronghold in regions where economic concerns remained paramount. Each state's outcome contributed to a broader narrative, with swing states once again proving to be decisive in shaping the path to the White House.

Chapter 6: State-by-State Analysis

Notable State Results and Regional Trends

The 2024 election revealed a landscape of distinct regional trends and shifting political alliances that underscored the evolving dynamics of American politics. Each state played a unique role in determining the final outcome, with results reflecting the concerns and priorities of diverse populations across the nation. This election showcased not only how demographics influenced results but also how specific issues resonated differently in each state. Economic conditions, social policies, and even local leadership contributed to the voting patterns seen in each region, creating a mosaic of political sentiment that reflected America's diversity.

The election results from the Midwest, for instance, showed the influence of economic concerns, particularly in states like Michigan, Wisconsin, and Ohio, where many voters were driven by issues surrounding job security, manufacturing, and trade policies. Trump's focus on reviving American industry and prioritising the domestic economy resonated strongly here, as he appealed to working-class voters who felt left behind by globalization and technological changes. The impact of these promises was evident in these states' voting results, where support for Trump remained strong, particularly in regions where manufacturing and industry have historically played a central role. Despite competition, Trump's message of economic revitalisation and protectionism struck a chord in these areas, resulting in significant support among traditional working-class communities.

However, coastal states such as California and New York largely maintained their historical preference for more progressive candidates, with voters prioritising issues like climate change, healthcare, and social justice. These states demonstrated strong support for candidates advocating for environmental protections, gender and racial equality, and expansive social policies. The urban centres within these states, characterised by diverse populations and progressive values, continued to be strongholds for candidates aligned with these issues.

This pattern underscores a longstanding trend where urban, coastal areas lean toward progressive policies, driven by younger, diverse, and more urbanized populations. The contrast between the concerns in these states and those in the Midwest reflected the wide range of priorities among American voters, highlighting the challenges of creating policies that address the needs of both rural and urban areas.

Southern states, including Texas and Florida, presented a mix of voting trends that underscored the region's shifting dynamics. Texas, long considered a Republican stronghold, saw changing patterns due to the rapid growth of urban areas like Austin, Houston, and Dallas, which have attracted younger, more diverse populations in recent years. This demographic shift has introduced more progressive voices into the political landscape, leading to closer races and increased political engagement in the state.

However, Trump maintained a strong base in more rural areas, where conservative values and concerns over immigration and economic policy continued to drive significant support. Florida, meanwhile, reinforced its status as a critical battleground state, with its diverse electorate reflecting a blend of conservative and progressive views, creating a tightly contested environment. Hispanic and Latino voters, particularly Cuban and Venezuelan communities, leaned toward Trump due to his stance on socialism and foreign policy in Latin America, adding complexity to Florida's political landscape.

Key Takeaways from Each State's Voting Outcome

Each state's voting outcome in the 2024 election provided key insights into the current political landscape and the forces shaping American society. One of the notable takeaways was the enduring strength of conservative sentiment in traditionally Republican states. Despite demographic shifts in certain areas, Trump was able to consolidate his base by focusing on policies that resonated with rural voters, blue-collar workers, and communities with strong cultural ties to conservative values.

This support proved to be crucial in securing victories in several swing states and demonstrated that his appeal among these groups remains strong, even as the nation becomes more politically divided. In states like Ohio and Iowa, where manufacturing and farming remain significant, Trump's focus on trade and economic protections contributed to his robust performance, reinforcing the importance of these states in his coalition.

The election also highlighted the growing influence of younger, progressive voters in urban centres and suburban areas, particularly in states with rapidly diversifying populations. States like Georgia and Arizona, which have historically leaned Republican, showed signs of shifting due to increasing engagement from younger voters and minorities who prioritised issues such as climate change, racial justice, and healthcare reform. The suburban vote in particular played a pivotal role in these regions, as more educated, affluent suburbanites expressed support for policies that aligned with social equality and environmental sustainability. These patterns suggest that states once considered solidly Republican may continue to see competitive races in future elections, as demographic shifts and changing values reshape the electorate.

Moreover, to demographic influences, key policy issues emerged as significant drivers of voter behavior, with different states prioritising distinct aspects of the candidates' platforms. In Pennsylvania and Michigan, for instance, voters expressed strong concerns about trade and economic security, favoring Trump's message of revitalising American manufacturing and protecting domestic jobs. Meanwhile, in states like Colorado and Oregon, where environmental issues have substantial local impact, there was a pronounced shift toward candidates advocating for climate action and environmental protections. This geographical divergence in policy priorities highlights the complexity of addressing a wide range of voter needs across the country, underscoring the importance of tailored messaging and targeted policies.

Another takeaway from the state-by-state results was the role of grassroots activism and voter mobilization efforts, which proved instrumental in increasing turnout among key groups. In states like Wisconsin and Nevada, both campaigns made extensive efforts to engage with minority communities, young voters, and working-class individuals, focusing on door-to-door outreach, community events, and social media campaigns to drive participation. This approach was particularly effective in regions where previous elections saw lower voter turnout, suggesting that active engagement and investment in local communities can significantly influence outcomes in tightly contested states. Grassroots efforts and local activism may become even more critical in future elections, as political campaigns recognise the value of building connections with voters at the community level.

The influence of independent voters and swing counties also stood out in the 2024 election. In states like Michigan, Pennsylvania, and Arizona, the decisions of independent voters were crucial in determining the final outcomes. Trump's campaign efforts to address economic concerns, combined with his direct messaging style, resonated with independents who may not be firmly aligned with either major party. Swing counties in these states, known for alternating between parties in different election cycles, became focal points for both campaigns, as each sought to win over undecided voters with appeals that addressed local concerns and emphasised pragmatic solutions.

The impact of these independent voters underscores the importance of messaging that can bridge ideological divides and appeal to a broader spectrum of Americans, especially in regions where party loyalty is less pronounced.

Chapter 7: Impact of Voter Sentiment and Media Influence

Role of Traditional and Social Media in Shaping Views

In the 2024 election, the role of media was more complex and influential than ever before, reflecting the transformation in how Americans consume information. Traditional media—such as newspapers, television, and radio—had once been the primary sources of news and political commentary. Yet, by 2024, social media platforms and online news outlets had gained significant ground, reshaping the way information spread and public opinion formed. This shift gave campaigns, candidates, and supporters a new level of access to voters, enabling them to bypass traditional filters and share messages directly with audiences. However, it also raised concerns over misinformation, polarization, and the potential manipulation of voter sentiment.

Traditional media outlets maintained their influence by providing a platform for in-depth political analysis, investigative reporting, and live election coverage. Major networks and newspapers still played a vital role in delivering information to the public, particularly for older generations who relied on these sources for trustworthy news. In the months leading up to the election, established media organisations conducted interviews, published op-eds, and hosted debates that framed key issues, giving candidates a platform to present their agendas to the nation. These outlets provided continuity, anchoring the election discourse in a professional setting that, for many, symbolized stability and reliability.

Yet, even as traditional media aimed to offer balanced coverage, there was a growing perception among many voters that these outlets were biased, often leaning toward specific ideological positions. This perception was particularly strong among Trump supporters, who felt that traditional media was more critical of their candidate than of his opponent. This sentiment drove Trump's supporters to seek alternative sources of information, especially on social media platforms, where they felt their views were better represented. Platforms like Facebook, Twitter, and Instagram, as well as alternative outlets like YouTube and various podcast channels, became essential spaces for political discourse, often presenting unfiltered opinions and rallying Trump's base with direct, passionate messaging.

Social media not only amplified political opinions but also fostered a sense of community among voters with similar views. Platforms allowed candidates and their supporters to connect in ways that were unthinkable in past elections, creating virtual spaces where information—often unverified—could circulate freely. Social media posts, live videos, and interactive content helped candidates reach millions of voters instantly. Donald Trump's campaign, in particular, utilized these platforms effectively, leveraging his social media presence to bypass traditional news cycles and speak directly to his followers. His posts, often pointed and provocative, engaged supporters and created a sense of direct access to their candidate, building a bond that traditional media rarely fostered.

This direct connection had a substantial impact on voter sentiment, as it allowed candidates to control the narrative around their campaigns. However, the speed and reach of social media also meant that misinformation could spread easily, potentially distorting public perceptions. Misleading posts, edited videos, and unverified reports quickly circulated across these platforms, shaping views in ways that were hard to counteract with facts. Efforts to label or correct misinformation were often met with resistance, as users questioned the motivations behind fact-checking initiatives. The sheer volume of information available, combined with selective exposure to like-minded content, created a polarising effect, where individuals became more entrenched in their views, often disregarding or distrusting opposing perspectives.

Public Sentiment and Key Influencers in the Election

Public sentiment in the 2024 election was a powerful, driving force shaped by deep concerns over the future of the country. Economic challenges, social issues, and cultural divides had created an electorate that was both highly engaged and polarised. Trump's supporters felt an urgent need to protect traditional values, prioritising issues such as job creation, national security, and limited government intervention. On the other hand, his opponents were motivated by concerns over social justice, climate change, and healthcare, seeing these as essential to building a more inclusive and progressive America. These differing priorities contributed to a sense of heightened emotion and urgency, as voters perceived the election as a decision between two distinct futures.

Social media influencers, pundits, and thought leaders played a significant role in shaping these sentiments, often acting as intermediaries between candidates and the public. Influencers with substantial followings on platforms like Instagram, Tikor, and Twitter took strong positions on the election, either endorsing candidates or sharing content that aligned with their views. These individuals were particularly influential among younger voters, who often looked to social media for insights and updates on current events. Influencers, both political and non-political, contributed to a highly charged atmosphere, using their platforms to highlight specific issues, promote voter engagement, and encourage activism. Their endorsements, opinions, and reposted content added to the visibility of the election, motivating followers to participate, donate, and vote.

Public figures from various fields—including entertainment, sports, and technology—also took clear stances, encouraging their audiences to vote and often voicing support for a particular candidate or cause. Figures such as Elon Musk, who has a vast following on social media, were particularly influential in drawing attention to the election and shaping public sentiment. These endorsements served as powerful tools for voter mobilization, as fans and followers often aligned their views with those of figures they admired. Trump's base, in particular, benefitted from high-profile supporters who consistently used their platforms to reinforce his message, creating a network of advocates who amplified his campaign themes to a wide audience.

However, the influence of these individuals was not without controversy. The sheer volume of opinions and endorsements, sometimes accompanied by misinformation, added a layer of complexity to the election. Social media algorithms played a role in amplifying content that garnered high engagement, often showing users posts that confirmed their existing beliefs. This created a feedback loop in which individuals primarily encountered views that matched their own, reinforcing biases and deepening divisions. The lack of exposure to balanced viewpoints contributed to an environment where many felt that only their perspective was legitimate, making it difficult for campaigns to reach across ideological divides.

Public sentiment in the 2024 election was also influenced by grassroots movements and citizen-led initiatives that grew out of frustration with traditional politics. These movements, often facilitated by social media, organised rallies, fundraisers, and voter registration drives, galvanizing communities around shared values and goals. The power of grassroots initiatives became evident as local leaders and organizers mobilized people who were otherwise disillusioned with the political process. This aspect of the election revealed an undercurrent of desire for change, as ordinary citizens stepped up to influence the narrative and encourage voter turnout.

The highly polarised atmosphere ultimately created an election season that was as much about personal identity as it was about policy. For many voters, their choice in 2024 felt like an affirmation of their values, beliefs, and vision for the country. Public sentiment, intensified by media influence and the personal stakes felt by many, led to an election where each vote symbolized more than just a political preference; it was a statement of individual and collective identity.

The impact of voter sentiment and media influence in the 2024 election cannot be overstated. The blending of traditional and social media created an environment where information—and misinformation—spread quickly, shaping public opinion in real-time. Social media's power to connect individuals, amplify voices, and build communities had both positive and negative effects, as it engaged voters and motivated action but also deepened divisions. The presence of key influencers and public figures added another layer of complexity, as their endorsements carried weight, mobilizing voters and reinforcing ideological divides. The election illustrated how the evolving landscape of media and public sentiment will continue to play a defining role in American politics, influencing not only how elections are conducted but also how voters perceive their role in the democratic process.

Chapter 8: Election Day and the Final Results

Key Events on Election Day

Election Day in 2024 unfolded with a unique mix of anticipation and tension. Citizens across the United States headed to polling stations early, while millions more cast their votes by mail or participated in early voting due to the expanded accessibility options that had emerged in recent years. From dawn to dusk, voters lined up at polling stations, with some regions experiencing higher-than-expected turnout and others noting a steadier flow of voters due to early voting options that had already reduced Election Day crowds. Key events during the day gave the public and the media plenty to discuss, as candidates, political analysts, and citizens kept a close eye on voting trends and emerging reports.

Throughout the day, unexpected events and logistical challenges unfolded. Some states experienced delays due to technical issues with voting machines or last-minute procedural changes, while other areas saw an unexpected surge in voter turnout that required extended hours at certain polling locations. Despite these occasional hiccups,

Election Day proceeded with a sense of unity, as Americans, regardless of political leanings, exercised their right to vote. Polling stations in pivotal swing states such as Pennsylvania, Arizona, and Georgia reported notably high turnout, underscoring the impact these states would have on the final outcome.

By midday, exit poll data started to trickle in, providing early insights into voter sentiment and the demographics shaping the election. Analysts noted significant shifts in voting patterns compared to previous years, with heightened engagement among young voters and minority groups, particularly in urban areas. The role of suburban and rural voters also emerged as critical, with both campaigns having invested significant resources in reaching these populations. As the day progressed, it became clear that the election would not yield immediate results, with both camps closely watching key counties in swing states, where the outcomes could tip the balance in either direction.

Breakdown of Final Results and Close Contests

As the final votes were counted, the 2024 election delivered a surprising and definitive outcome. Donald Trump emerged victorious, reclaiming the presidency with a strong showing in key battleground states. The breakdown of results underscored several critical trends that had been developing in American politics over recent years. Trump's success hinged on strong turnout from his base, particularly in rural areas and traditionally conservative regions. His campaign's messaging around economic stability, national security, and preserving American values resonated with a broad segment of voters who felt overlooked in recent years.

Swing states proved decisive in delivering Trump's victory. States like Pennsylvania, Michigan, and Wisconsin, often considered bellwethers in presidential elections, tilted in Trump's favour by narrow margins, demonstrating his campaign's effective targeting of specific voter blocs. Additionally, states such as Florida and Ohio, which had leaned towards Trump in previous elections, delivered substantial margins, further solidifying his path to the presidency. In states where the races were particularly close, recounts and legal challenges emerged, but the margins ultimately held firm, confirming Trump's win.

In several key states, the margins were razor-thin, with just a few thousand votes making the difference. Arizona and Georgia, for example, saw extremely close contests, leading to intense scrutiny and recount efforts. These states highlighted the divided nature of the electorate, where both urban and rural areas brought in contrasting perspectives. In Georgia, Atlanta and its surrounding suburbs leaned heavily towards Trump's opponent, while rural counties swung towards Trump, creating a close contest that ultimately fell in his favour. Arizona followed a similar pattern, with Phoenix and Tucson contrasting with more conservative rural areas, leading to a final result that underscored the balance of power between urban and rural interests.

The final results also shed light on shifting demographics within the voter base. Trump performed surprisingly well with certain minority groups, including Hispanic and African American voters in specific regions, challenging the conventional assumptions about voting patterns. His success in reaching these demographics reflected a complex picture of American society, where economic issues, cultural values, and social concerns intersected in unexpected ways. These shifts in voting patterns indicated a nuanced political landscape, one that is becoming increasingly difficult to predict as voters align less strictly along traditional party lines and more with candidates who address their immediate concerns and aspirations.

As Election Day came to a close and the results were finalized, the 2024 election left a lasting impression on the American public. It highlighted the ongoing changes in the electorate, the importance of targeted messaging, and the role of grassroots mobilization. The close contests in numerous states underscored the deep divisions within the country, yet also emphasised the power of the democratic process. In a political landscape where each vote counted more than ever, the 2024 election became a testament to the resilience of American democracy and the enduring commitment of its citizens to make their voices heard.

Chapter 9: Reactions from Both Sides

Reactions from Trump Supporters and Opponents

The reaction to the 2024 election results was one of heightened passion, as Americans across the political spectrum took to social media, news outlets, and public gatherings to voice their views. For Trump supporters, the victory was celebrated as a return to what they saw as "America First" principles and a leader who could reinstate a sense of stability and pride in the nation. In the days following the election, rallies and gatherings formed across many cities and towns where Trump supporters waved American flags, chanted campaign slogans, and echoed Trump's promise to restore traditional values and economic strength.

Many supporters felt that Trump's victory represented not only a return to power but also a validation of their frustrations with recent shifts in American policy and culture. This election, in their view, was a critical moment to steer the country back toward the principles they believed in, such as strong national borders, economic revitalisation, and a clear stance on global issues.

For these supporters, the win was seen as a collective victory. Many had been vocal in their criticism of policies that they felt had neglected the needs of working-class Americans and allowed issues like inflation, unemployment, and crime to fester.

Trump's messaging had consistently assured them that he would address these concerns head-on, creating what they believed would be a safer, more prosperous America. His promises to reduce government intervention, lower taxes, and put American interests first resonated strongly, especially among rural and industrial communities that felt marginalised. Celebrations took place not only in expected strongholds but even in suburban and urban areas where his message had reached a diverse array of supporters. For them, this was not just a political victory but a vindication of their belief in the need for a stronger, more assertive government that prioritises American citizens.

On the other hand, reactions from Trump's opponents were marked by disappointment, fear, and even anger. Many of those opposed to Trump's return to office had voiced concerns throughout the campaign about the potential repercussions of his leadership. For them, Trump's victory signalled a setback on several fronts, particularly concerning social justice, climate change, and international relations. Many feared that his administration would reverse recent strides made in these areas, shifting policies in ways they believed would harm both the country and the planet. Public expressions of opposition were immediate, with organised protests and vigils held in major cities. Social media became a hub for these voices, with users posting messages of concern and solidarity, hoping to find ways to resist what they perceived as a rollback of critical rights and protections.

However, to protests, many of Trump's opponents turned their focus toward advocating for local and state-level initiatives, believing that grassroots efforts could counterbalance federal policies they disagreed with. For these individuals, the election outcome represented a call to action. Community organisations and activists vowed to intensify their efforts, aiming to protect social and environmental programs that they worried might be at risk under the new administration. Their reaction was not simply a rejection of Trump as an individual but a broader critique of the policies and perspectives he represented. This divide between supporters and opponents highlighted the polarization that had become a defining feature of American politics, with each side viewing the election as either a necessary correction or a dangerous regression.

International Responses to the U.S. Election Outcome

The 2024 U.S. election results were closely watched by countries around the world, with reactions reflecting the global implications of America's political direction. Allies and rivals alike responded to Trump's victory with a mix of optimism, caution, and speculation. For many European countries, Trump's return raised questions about the future of international alliances, particularly with NATO and the European Union. While some leaders expressed congratulations, there was an undercurrent of uncertainty about how Trump's foreign policy would affect global stability and cooperation. Trump's stance on issues like defence spending, trade agreements, and climate change had previously led to strained relations with several European nations, and his return prompted discussions about how these alliances would evolve. Leaders in Europe held discussions on preparing for potential shifts in trade, security, and climate policies, knowing that Trump's approach could differ sharply from recent U.S. strategies.

In Asia, responses were equally varied. Countries like Japan and South Korea, traditional allies of the United States, issued cautious statements of congratulations, mindful of the impact that Trump's administration might have on security dynamics in the region. Trump's previous policies in Asia had focused on confronting issues related to China and North Korea, and his return to office renewed speculation about how he might handle these relationships. China's response, meanwhile, was more reserved, with state media issuing cautious statements about the need for cooperation despite ideological differences.

Analysts speculated that Trump's administration would continue a firm stance on trade and technology disputes, which had been a significant source of tension between the two superpowers. In South Asia, where issues of trade and security also loom large, countries monitored the situation closely, recognising the potential for both challenges and opportunities under the new administration.

Latin America's reaction was particularly significant, as Trump's policies on immigration and trade had long affected the region. Governments in countries like Mexico and Brazil responded with mixed emotions, anticipating potential shifts in policies that could impact migration, border security, and trade relations.

Trump's prior focus on immigration control and his plans to reinforce border security created apprehension among Latin American leaders, as they prepared for potential challenges in diplomatic and economic relations. At the same time, some leaders saw opportunities to engage in new trade discussions that could benefit their economies if approached strategically. The sentiment in Latin America reflected both a need for cautious diplomacy and an interest in protecting their national interests amid anticipated policy changes.

Beyond specific regions, international organisations such as the United Nations and the World Health Organization also prepared for potential shifts in

U.S. involvement. Trump's stance on multilateral organisations had previously been sceptical, with a preference for bilateral agreements and a "U.S.-first" approach. This perspective had led to decreased funding and cooperation in areas like climate change and health initiatives, and Trump's victory raised questions about future engagement. These organisations anticipated that the U.S. might again adopt a more self-focused stance, potentially reducing collaborative efforts in areas of global concern. Nonetheless, they expressed hope for continued dialogue, recognising the importance of U.S. involvement in achieving long-term global objectives.

The response from America's international allies and competitors underscores the extent to which U.S. politics influences global affairs. Trump's return to the White House was met with a blend of optimism, wariness, and strategic recalibration among world leaders. For some, his victory signalled a possible shift towards more assertive policies that could redefine international relationships. For others, it raised concerns about potential disruptions in established alliances and cooperation on issues of shared importance.

This complex reaction reflects the global stakes of American elections, as countries around the world adapt to changes in U.S. leadership that could influence everything from trade to environmental policies. The 2024 election demonstrated that America's political choices continue to resonate far beyond its borders, shaping a world that remains closely attuned to the direction set by its leaders.

Chapter 10: What Trump's Win Means for America

Policy Agenda and Expected Legislative Focus

Donald Trump's return to the White House in 2024 set the stage for a new era of policy direction, driven by his ambitious agenda and the support of his committed base. His win highlighted a demand for a shift in the direction of American politics, one that aims to address economic stability, national security, and the foundational values that Trump champions. As he settles into his second term, his policy agenda is poised to reflect the priorities he has consistently voiced throughout his campaign. Central to his legislative focus are issues like economic reform, immigration control, healthcare reorganization, and law enforcement.

Trump's economic agenda, which remains a cornerstone of his platform, is expected to prioritise tax reforms, deregulation, and policies aimed at boosting domestic industry. Trump's philosophy emphasises a free-market approach, aimed at reducing federal government intervention to enable businesses to grow more freely. His administration is likely to push for tax cuts aimed at corporations and middle-income earners, with the belief that these cuts will fuel job growth, increase wages, and strengthen American industries. This approach resonates strongly with his supporters, many of whom feel that previous policies have stifled economic opportunity and favored international interests over domestic ones.

Alongside economic reform, Trump's legislative focus is set to intensify on immigration. He has made clear that he views immigration control as essential to national security and economic stability. During his first term, Trump implemented stricter immigration measures, and this time around, he is expected to take a more comprehensive approach, focusing on policies to curb illegal immigration, streamline deportation processes, and secure the U.S. border. His administration's stance on immigration appeals to his base's concerns about the impact of illegal immigration on jobs, wages, and resources. Proposed measures could include increased funding for border security, a more robust legal framework for enforcement, and stronger pathways to ensure only legal immigration is pursued.

Healthcare reform is another significant area where Trump intends to leave his mark.

His administration has long been critical of the Affordable Care Act, and his return to office provides an opportunity to revisit and reshape the national healthcare system. Trump's vision for healthcare includes reducing government involvement and promoting private sector competition to drive down costs. This approach is intended to increase accessibility while maintaining quality, although it has sparked debate over how such changes would impact Americans who depend on government-subsidized healthcare. Nonetheless, Trump's administration views these changes as a path to a more sustainable system, where healthcare costs are managed through competition rather than extensive federal oversight.

In domestic policy, Trump has also shown a strong commitment to law enforcement, advocating for policies that promote "law and order." His administration's stance reflects his belief that a stable society is essential to economic and social progress. Trump's legislative agenda is likely to include measures that increase support for law enforcement agencies, bolster resources for policing, and implement stricter penalties for violent crimes. For Trump and his supporters, these policies are seen as vital to addressing concerns about rising crime rates, particularly in urban areas. By focusing on law enforcement, he aims to establish a sense of security and reinforce a societal structure that his base believes has been undermined in recent years.

Anticipated Changes in Domestic and Foreign Policy

Trump's win in 2024 also signifies significant changes in both domestic and foreign policy. On the domestic front, his administration's focus on economic and regulatory reforms aims to shift the country toward a pro-business, economically driven agenda. With his return to the White House, Trump is expected to continue reducing federal oversight in various sectors, promoting energy independence, and encouraging the growth of American industries. His administration is likely to champion energy policies that prioritise fossil fuel production, including oil and natural gas, as part of his strategy to bolster domestic resources and reduce dependency on foreign energy. This direction contrasts sharply with previous policies focused on renewable energy, underscoring Trump's commitment to traditional energy sources as key drivers of the American economy.

Trump's stance on environmental regulations further reflects his administration's emphasis on economic growth. He has often criticised what he perceives as restrictive environmental policies, arguing that they inhibit industrial development and job creation. In his second term, Trump's administration is expected to roll back several regulations that he believes hinder the growth of industries such as mining, oil drilling, and manufacturing. This approach aligns with his pro-business philosophy, which prioritises economic opportunity over regulatory constraints. His supporters view this shift as essential to restoring American manufacturing and ensuring that economic policies support working-class communities that rely on these industries for employment.

On the foreign policy front, Trump's return to the White House is likely to mark a shift towards a more unilateral approach, focusing on American interests over multilateral agreements. His administration has consistently emphasised the importance of sovereignty, economic nationalism, and a cautious approach to foreign alliances. Trump's "America First" doctrine underscores his belief that the U.S. should prioritise its own interests, particularly in areas of trade, defence, and foreign aid. He is likely to continue negotiating trade deals that he believes will strengthen the American economy, with a focus on securing advantageous terms that benefit American workers and industries. This approach may lead to renegotiations of existing agreements and a cautious approach to entering new multilateral deals.

In defence policy, Trump's administration is expected to take a strong stance, focusing on military investment and a robust defence strategy. Trump has consistently advocated for a well-funded military, viewing it as essential to protecting American interests and maintaining global stability. His administration is likely to pursue increased defence spending to modernise the military, enhance cybersecurity, and strengthen national security. This direction reflects his commitment to safeguarding the U.S. from potential threats and ensuring that the country maintains a dominant position in global security matters. Trump's approach to defence aligns with his broader vision of asserting American power on the international stage, a strategy that he argues is necessary to counter adversaries and protect national sovereignty.

One of the most anticipated changes in foreign relations under Trump's administration is his approach to allies and international institutions. Trump's previous term was marked by criticism of NATO, the United Nations, and other multilateral organisations, and he is expected to adopt a similar stance in his second term. Trump's administration views alliances as beneficial only when they align with American interests, and he has been outspoken about his desire for allies to contribute more substantially to collective defence efforts. His return to office may lead to renewed calls for NATO members to increase their defence spending, as well as efforts to restructure the U.S.'s role within other international bodies. This approach reflects Trump's belief in a more self-reliant and independent America, one that does not shoulder disproportionate burdens in global affairs.

Trump's second term is also likely to reshape U.S. relations with adversaries, particularly with nations like China, Russia, and Iran. His administration has taken a firm stance on issues such as trade imbalances, intellectual property rights, and geopolitical influence, especially with China. Trump's approach to China, in particular, is expected to remain assertive, focusing on reducing economic dependency and addressing security concerns related to technology and trade. His administration is likely to pursue policies aimed at containing China's influence in Asia and globally, including economic sanctions, trade restrictions, and strategic alliances with regional partners. This stance reflects Trump's commitment to protecting American interests against what he sees as economic and political threats posed by rival nations.

Chapter 11: Challenges and Opportunities in a New Era

Obstacles Facing the New Administration

As the new administration takes office, it faces a range of significant obstacles, many of which are rooted in the polarised political landscape and the complex challenges left behind by previous years. The economic landscape, for instance, is one of the most immediate and pressing concerns. Rising inflation, wage stagnation, and a labor market struggling to find equilibrium have created a sense of economic insecurity for millions of Americans.

The administration's ability to address these economic challenges will likely shape public perception early on, as citizens look for relief from the pressures of everyday expenses. Finding a balance between stimulating growth and managing inflation is a delicate task that requires not only sound policy but a strategic approach to economic communication. If mishandled, these issues could quickly erode public confidence, especially among those who were hoping for swift change.

Another obstacle facing the administration is the ongoing need for healthcare reform. The healthcare system in the United States has long been a source of contention, and while recent years have seen progress in expanding access, millions remain uninsured or face prohibitively high costs.

This administration will be challenged to navigate these complexities while balancing the demands for affordable healthcare with the need for sustainable government spending. There is growing public pressure to improve healthcare options, lower prescription drug prices, and make mental health support more accessible. However, healthcare reform is notoriously complex, and any effort to address it will likely encounter resistance from both private industry and political opponents who argue that over-regulation could stifle innovation.

Environmental policy also poses a significant challenge, particularly as climate change remains a prominent concern among voters. The administration is expected to face pressure from both sides: environmental advocates pushing for aggressive climate policies, and industrial and energy sectors concerned about regulatory burdens that might hinder economic growth. Striking a balance between protecting the environment and supporting economic interests is no easy feat, especially with such diverse opinions on the best path forward. The administration's stance on environmental issues, particularly in areas like renewable energy investment, fossil fuel regulation, and carbon emissions targets, will be closely scrutinised by both domestic and international observers.

Furthermore, the administration must address immigration policy, a deeply divisive issue with strong opinions on both sides. The need for secure borders and effective immigration systems is a common thread in American politics, but the methods for achieving these goals are heavily debated. The administration faces the task of balancing border security with humane and fair immigration practices, all while managing the expectations of a public that is divided on this issue. Failure to find a workable solution could lead to further polarization, as supporters demand stronger measures and critics call for compassion and inclusivity.

Finally, the political climate itself is one of the greatest challenges. The current atmosphere of partisanship makes it difficult for any administration to govern effectively, as even seemingly minor issues can quickly become political battlegrounds. The administration will need to find ways to build bridges and foster dialogue, not only to pass legislation but to rebuild public trust in government institutions. The lack of cooperation between political parties in recent years has eroded confidence in Washington, and the new administration faces the daunting task of restoring that trust. Whether it can succeed will depend largely on its approach to leadership and its ability to navigate the complexities of a divided nation.

Areas for Potential Bipartisan Collaboration

Despite the challenges, there are several areas where the administration may find opportunities for bipartisan collaboration, offering a chance to bridge divides and work toward shared goals. Infrastructure investment is one of the most promising areas for cooperation, as both parties recognise the importance of updating and expanding America's aging infrastructure. Roads, bridges, public transportation, and digital infrastructure are in dire need of repair, and investment in these areas could create jobs, boost the economy, and improve quality of life. The administration's commitment to revitalising infrastructure may provide an opening to work across the aisle, as these projects are widely viewed as essential and less ideologically charged than other policy areas. A successful infrastructure initiative could not only enhance the nation's economic resilience but also demonstrate that cooperation is still possible in Washington.

Education reform is another promising area for bipartisan efforts, particularly when it comes to issues like vocational training, community college funding, and digital literacy. As the nature of work continues to evolve, both parties recognise the need for an education system that prepares students for a diverse range of careers. Expanding access to vocational training and investing in technical education could provide a pathway for millions of Americans to find stable employment in a rapidly changing job market. Moreover, as digital technology becomes increasingly integral to daily life, there is bipartisan interest in ensuring that all Americans have access to digital skills training, which can reduce barriers to entry in many sectors. Education reform, therefore, represents an opportunity for collaboration that could have a profound and lasting impact on the nation's workforce.

Healthcare reform, while complex and challenging, also presents opportunities for bipartisan progress in specific areas. Both parties, for example, share concerns about the high cost of prescription drugs and the need to address the opioid crisis. By focusing on these targeted issues, the administration may find common ground that could lead to incremental improvements in the healthcare system. Efforts to reduce drug prices, increase access to mental health services, and expand addiction treatment programs are likely to receive support from across the political spectrum. While sweeping healthcare reform may be difficult to achieve, these smaller steps could make a meaningful difference and demonstrate the potential for bipartisan cooperation.

Another area ripe for collaboration is criminal justice reform. Recent years have seen growing recognition on both sides of the aisle that the criminal justice system needs reform, particularly in areas like sentencing laws, rehabilitation programs, and reintegration support for former inmates. Policymakers are increasingly aware that a balanced approach to justice is essential for reducing recidivism and improving community safety. The administration could work with lawmakers from both parties to support reforms that reduce prison populations, provide better support for those re-entering society, and address racial disparities within the system. Criminal justice reform has the potential to improve lives and communities, and a bipartisan approach could help ensure these changes are implemented in a sustainable, balanced way.

Finally, cybersecurity and technology regulation offer promising areas for bipartisan work, as both parties recognise the importance of protecting the nation's digital infrastructure. Cybersecurity is not only a national security issue but also a matter of protecting citizens' privacy and securing critical systems from foreign interference. The administration could work with Congress to develop regulations that protect data privacy, prevent cyberattacks, and promote responsible technology use.

This is especially important as technological advances continue to outpace regulatory frameworks, creating risks for both individuals and organisations. Bipartisan support for improved cybersecurity measures would help secure America's digital landscape and build resilience against emerging threats.

In a new era defined by both challenges and opportunities, the administration's ability to navigate these complex issues will likely define its legacy. While there are numerous obstacles to overcome, the potential for bipartisan collaboration offers a hopeful path forward. By focusing on areas where common ground can be found, the administration has the opportunity to not only address pressing issues but also rebuild public trust and demonstrate that productive governance is still possible.

The choices made in these early years will shape the nation's trajectory and lay the foundation for future progress, highlighting the importance of leadership that is both visionary and pragmatic. As the administration tackles these challenges, it will be tested, but in those tests lies the potential to bring about meaningful change and unity in a nation eager for solutions.

Chapter 12: The Future of American Politics Post-2024

Implications for Future Presidential Elections

The 2024 election has undoubtedly reshaped the landscape of American politics, setting precedents and creating a foundation that will likely influence future presidential elections. In many ways, it signalled a new era in which traditional approaches to campaigning and governing may be sidelined in favour of more dynamic, targeted, and responsive strategies. For future elections, candidates and parties alike will need to consider the shifts seen in 2024, particularly the ways in which voter expectations and engagement have evolved. In an age where information flows rapidly and voters have access to more data, analysis, and opinion than ever before, future candidates will likely find themselves under intense scrutiny, with their policies and platforms dissected and discussed in real time.

One key implication of the 2024 election is the increasing importance of personalization in political outreach. Both major campaigns demonstrated the power of data-driven, highly targeted messaging that speaks directly to the concerns of specific voter segments. This trend suggests that future presidential hopefuls will need to adopt similar strategies, understanding the unique needs and expectations of various groups within the electorate. Blanket promises and generic platforms may no longer suffice, as voters are looking for politicians who can connect with them on a more personal level. Campaigns that harness data analytics, social media insights, and micro-targeted advertising are likely to be the norm, as they allow candidates to build nuanced strategies that cater to different demographics and regions.

The 2024 election also underscored the impact of social media as a powerful tool in shaping voter perceptions and sentiment. Future candidates will need to be exceptionally savvy in navigating online platforms, understanding that these spaces are where many voters form their opinions and build their trust—or distrust—toward candidates. Social media will likely remain a central battleground, where campaigns compete to define narratives, highlight key messages, and counter misinformation. In this environment, a candidate's digital presence will need to be as carefully crafted as their public appearances, and a keen understanding of social media dynamics will be essential. The ability to respond quickly and authentically on digital platforms could become a deciding factor, with voters expecting transparency and real-time engagement.

Also, future presidential elections may reflect the rising importance of independent and third-party candidates. In 2024, there was a noticeable increase in disillusionment with the traditional two-party system, leading some voters to explore alternative options. If this trend continues, we may see a shift toward more viable third-party candidates, or at least a stronger call for alternative voices within the political spectrum. Future elections could see a more fragmented voter base, with candidates needing to appeal to an electorate that is less predictable and more diverse in its affiliations. The concept of party loyalty may become less relevant as voters prioritize individual values and policies over traditional party lines, forcing candidates to build coalitions that cross established boundaries.

Shifting Dynamics Within the Major Political Parties

The 2024 election has not only influenced the electorate but has also triggered significant shifts within both the Democratic and Republican parties. Within the Republican Party, Trump's return and subsequent victory have solidified his influence, marking a continued shift toward populist conservatism. This has implications for the party's identity and the types of candidates it will attract in future cycles.

Trump's approach, characterised by a blend of nationalism, anti-establishment rhetoric, and direct appeals to working-class voters, has reshaped the GOP's priorities and base. Moving forward, the party will likely see candidates who emulate Trump's style and focus on policies that resonate with his core supporters. However, this alignment with Trumping populism may also alienate moderate Republicans and independents, leading to potential internal conflicts as the party navigates its future direction.

The Democratic Party, meanwhile, faces its own challenges and opportunities following the 2024 election. The party's strategy of appealing to progressive values and diverse voter groups, particularly young voters, minority communities, and urban populations, remains a defining feature. However, the close results of the election have prompted questions within the party about whether its current platform is adequately broad to appeal to a wider segment of the electorate. The Democrats are likely to undergo internal debates about the extent to which they should embrace progressive policies versus adopting a more moderate approach that could appeal to swing voters. This internal balancing act will be crucial as the party seeks to maintain unity while still appealing to a diverse base with varying expectations and demands.

The 2024 election may also lead to increased polarization within both parties, as factions with differing ideologies attempt to steer the direction of their respective parties. Within the Republican Party, there are tensions between traditional conservatives and the newer populist wing, each advocating for different policy priorities and visions for the party's future. Traditional conservatives may feel that their influence is waning as the party leans more heavily into populism, while the populist wing, emboldened by Trump's victory, seeks to further its influence.

This dynamic could lead to internal power struggles as the GOP tries to reconcile these competing interests and define its identity moving forward.

Similarly, the Democratic Party faces the possibility of increasing polarization, particularly between its progressive wing and more moderate factions. Progressive Democrats, who champion bold reforms in areas such as healthcare, climate action, and social justice, may push for the party to adopt a more transformative agenda. However, moderate Democrats may argue for a more centrist approach that focuses on incremental changes and appeals to a broader coalition of voters. This ideological tension could lead to debates within the party about the best path forward, with both sides seeking to shape the party's platform and identity in a way that reflects their vision.

The 2024 election also highlighted the growing role of independent groups and political action committees (PACs) in shaping party dynamics. Both parties saw a surge in support from outside organisations, which played a significant role in funding campaigns, influencing voter perceptions, and advocating for specific issues. This trend suggests that in the future, both the Democratic and Republican parties may rely increasingly on these groups to mobilise support and resources. However, this reliance could lead to further fragmentation, as these groups often represent niche interests that may not align perfectly with the party's broader goals. The influence of these groups could complicate party unity, as elected officials may feel pressured to cater to the demands of outside interests rather than adhering to a cohesive party platform.

In the aftermath of the 2024 election, both parties face a period of introspection and adjustment as they assess the changing political landscape. For the Republican Party, the challenge will be to consolidate Trump's influence while addressing the needs of traditional conservatives and expanding its appeal to independents and moderate voters. For the Democratic Party, the focus may shift toward building a platform that unites progressive ideals with pragmatic approaches that can win over undecided voters. Both parties will likely need to embrace flexibility and adaptability as they navigate these shifting dynamics, understanding that the electorate's priorities and expectations are evolving.

As the political parties redefine themselves, the future of American politics will likely be marked by a greater emphasis on individuality and issue-based coalitions, as opposed to strict party loyalty. Voters have shown a growing willingness to support candidates who address their specific concerns, even if those candidates fall outside the traditional party lines. This shift toward individualized politics could lead to more diverse candidate pools, with parties feeling pressured to support individuals who represent a broad array of viewpoints and values. The era of rigid two-party dominance may gradually give way to a more flexible political environment, where the emphasis is placed on ideas and results rather than party allegiance.

Conclusion: A Defining Election

Long-Term Implications for American Democracy

The 2024 U.S. Presidential Election was a defining moment in American history, a turning point that underscored the profound ideological divides within the country and revealed the evolving landscape of modern democracy. More than just a contest between two candidates, this election laid bare the issues, sentiments, and forces shaping American society today and offered a glimpse into the future trajectory of its political system. As the dust settles, it's clear that the impacts of this election will extend far beyond the immediate policy shifts of the next four years, influencing how Americans engage with their government, how they perceive their civic responsibilities, and how future elections will be conducted and contested.

One of the most enduring implications of the 2024 election is the heightened role of technology and social media in shaping voter opinion. This election demonstrated the unprecedented power of data analytics, social media algorithms, and digital platforms in reaching and mobilizing voters.

Campaigns harnessed these tools to fine-tune messages, target specific demographics, and amplify voices that aligned with their agendas. While these strategies have brought a new level of engagement, they have also deepened echo chambers, allowing voters to curate their information streams and reinforcing divisions within the electorate. As a result, the future of American democracy will likely grapple with questions about the role of technology, the need for transparency in data usage, and the ethical considerations surrounding targeted political messaging.

Moreover, the 2024 election has revealed a pressing need to address the widening ideological gap among Americans. The sharp contrast in priorities—between voters who value economic and national security issues, and those focused on social justice and environmental concerns—highlights the challenge of fostering unity in a diverse, pluralistic society. This polarization, intensified by the election, underscores the importance of promoting constructive dialogue and finding common ground. As future administrations work to address this divide, the long-term health of American democracy may depend on the ability to build bridges between opposing viewpoints and foster a culture of tolerance and understanding, even when disagreement is inevitable.

Another lasting impact of the 2024 election lies in the shift of power dynamics within political parties. The election revealed a significant transformation within both the Republican and Democratic bases, with each side facing internal shifts and realignments. Trump's victory demonstrated the continued influence of populist sentiment within the Republican Party, as well as a growing preference for anti-establishment rhetoric and a strong "America First" stance. Meanwhile, the Democratic Party faced a renewed call for progressive reforms from its younger, more diverse base, highlighting the challenge of reconciling progressive ideals with the party's more moderate members. This realignment signals an ongoing evolution within both parties, one that will shape not only their policies but their strategies and identity moving forward.

The 2024 election also re-emphasized the role of grassroots movements and voter activism, a trend that has grown over the last decade. From climate activists and social justice organisations to groups advocating for economic reforms, grassroots movements proved to be powerful forces that shaped the electoral narrative and influenced the priorities of candidates. These movements mobilized millions, particularly among younger voters, who demanded accountability from their leaders and actively sought systemic change. The success of grassroots activism in the 2024 election sets a precedent for future elections, demonstrating the potential of organised, issue-focused campaigns to influence policy and drive voter engagement. As American democracy moves forward, these movements will continue to be an essential part of the political fabric, pushing for reforms and holding elected officials accountable to the needs of the people.

The Place of the 2024 Election in Political History

As historians and political analysts reflect on the 2024 election, it will likely hold a significant place in the story of American democracy, marked by its unique context, its ideological stakes, and its far-reaching consequences. This election can be seen as a reflection of the deep transformations that have taken place in American society, highlighting shifts in demographics, values, and expectations of leadership. The 2024 election will be remembered not only for the candidates and the policies they championed but for what it revealed about the American people—their hopes, their fears, and their vision for the future.

One of the defining features of the 2024 election was the return of Donald Trump to the national stage, a move that defied historical norms and challenged traditional expectations. Rarely does a former president seek re-election after a break from office, making Trump's return a remarkable event that captured the world's attention. His re-emergence reignited debates about the role of populism in American politics and demonstrated the enduring appeal of his message among a significant portion of the population. In this sense, the 2024 election will likely be studied as a case of political resilience and the power of personal brand, underscoring how a leader can maintain influence and support even after leaving office.

The 2024 election also stands out as a turning point in how campaigns are run, marking a shift toward highly personalized and data-driven strategies.

Future historians may view this election as a watershed moment in the digitization of democracy, where the use of targeted advertising, algorithms, and social media influence reached new heights. This trend raises important questions about the future of elections, including issues of privacy, information integrity, and the ethical boundaries of voter manipulation. As political campaigns continue to embrace technology, the 2024 election may serve as both a blueprint and a cautionary tale, illustrating the potential of digital tools to engage voters while also exposing the risks of creating isolated information bubbles.

In the broader narrative of political history, the 2024 election will also be remembered for the way it highlighted ongoing demographic shifts in the U.S. The election saw increased participation from minority groups, younger voters, and new citizens, all of whom contributed to shaping the outcome. This shift in the electorate reflects America's changing population and signals a future where these groups will continue to play an influential role in elections. The mobilization of diverse voter blocs, each with distinct priorities and values, underscores the need for political parties to adapt and evolve. As historians look back, they may view the 2024 election as a moment when the nation's demographic future became an undeniable force in its politics.

Furthermore, the 2024 election exposed the strengths and vulnerabilities of the American electoral system. Despite technological advancements, the election process faced challenges, from disinformation campaigns to concerns about the security of digital voting systems. These issues brought renewed attention to the integrity of the electoral process and emphasised the need for robust safeguards. Future political historians may see the 2024 election as a critical point that prompted reforms aimed at ensuring transparency, security, and trust in American democracy. This election may ultimately be regarded as a catalyst for revisiting and strengthening the democratic institutions that underpin the nation's political stability.

Looking back, the 2024 election holds lessons and insights that will resonate well into the future. It serves as a reminder of the power of democratic participation, the importance of civic engagement, and the impact of individual voices in shaping the course of history. While the immediate outcomes will undoubtedly shape policy and governance in the years to come, the election's true legacy will lie in its place as a symbol of American democracy in action. It exemplifies both the challenges and the promise of a system that empowers citizens to choose their leaders and to influence their nation's direction.

As the 2024 election takes its place in the annals of political history, it leaves behind a complex legacy. It reflects a nation at a crossroads, grappling with profound changes and searching for a path forward that reconciles its diverse perspectives. The election's impact will likely extend beyond any one administration, shaping the discourse, priorities, and values of American politics for years to come. In time, the lessons learned from this defining election will continue to inform and inspire, offering a blueprint for navigating the complexities of modern democracy and underscoring the resilience and adaptability of the American people.

Printed in Great Britain
by Amazon